CALIFORNIA
NATIVE AMERICAN TRIBES

GABRIELINO TRIBE

by

Mary Null Boulé

Book Six in a series of twenty-six

Dear Reader,

You will find an outline of this chapter's important topics at the back of the booklet. It is there for you to use in writing a report or giving an oral report on this tribe.

If you first read the booklet completely, then you can use the outline as a guide to write your report in your own words, instead of copying sentences from the chapter.

Good luck, read carefully,
and use your own words.

MNB

Cover Illustration: Daniel Liddell

GABRIELINO TRIBE

by
Mary Null Boulé

Illustrated by
Daniel Liddell

Merryant Publishing
Vashon, Washington

Book Number Six in a series of twenty-six

This series is dedicated to Virginia Harding, whose editing expertise and friendship brought this project to fruition.

Library of Congress Catalog Card Number: 92-61897

ISBN: 1-877599-30-1

Copyright © 1992, Merryant Publishing

7615 S.W. 257th St., Vashon, WA 98070.

FOREWORD

Native American people of the United States are often living their lives away from major cities and away from what we call the mainstream of life. It is, then, interesting to learn of the important part these remote tribal members play in our everyday lives.

More than 60% of our foods come from the ancient Native American's diet. Farming methods of today also can be traced back to how tribal women grew crops of corn and grain. Many of our present day ideas of democracy have been taken from tribal governments. Even some 1,500 Native American words are found in our English language today.

Fur traders bought furs from tribal hunters for small amounts of money, sold them to Europeans and Asians for a great deal of money, and became rich. Using their money to buy land and to build office buildings, some traders started

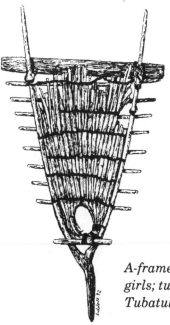

business corporations which are now the base of our country's economy.

There has never been enough credit given to these early Americans who took such good care of our country when it was still in their care. The time has come to realize tribal contributions to our society today and to give Native Americans not only the credit, but the respect due them.

Mary Boulé

A-frame cradle for girls; tule matting. Tubatulabal tribe.

GENERAL INFORMATION

Out of Asia, many thousands of years ago, came Wanderers. Some historians think they were the first people to set foot on our western hemisphere. These Wanderers had walked, step by step, onto our part of the earth while hunting and gathering food. They probably never even knew they had moved from one continent to another as they made their way across a land bridge, a narrow strip of land between Siberia and what is now Russia, and the state of Alaska.

Historians do not know exactly how long ago the Wanderers might have crossed the land bridge. Some of them say 35,000 years ago. What historians do know is that these people slowly moved down onto land that we now call the United States of America. Today it would be very hard to follow their footsteps, for the land bridge has been covered with sea water since the thawing of the ice age.

Those Wanderers who made their way to California were very lucky, indeed. California was a land with good weather most of the year and was filled with plenty of plant and animal foods for them to eat.

The Wanderers who became California's Native Americans did not organize into large tribes like the rest of the North American tribes. Instead, they divided into groups, or tribelets, sometimes having as many as 250 people. A tribelet could number as few as three, to as many as thirty villages located close to each other. Some tribelets had only one chief, a leader who lived in the largest village. Many tribes had a chief for each village. Some leaders had no real power but were thought to be wise. Tribal members always listened with respect to what their chief had to say.

From 20 to 100 people could be living in one village, which usually had several houses. In most cases, these groups of people were related to each other. From five to ten people of one family lived in one house. For instance, a mother, a father, two or three children, a grandmother, or aunt or daughter-in-law might live together.

Village members together would own the land important to them for their well-being. Their land might include oak trees with precious acorns, streams and rivers, and plants which were good to eat. Streams and rivers were especially important to a tribe's quality of life. Water drew animals to it; that meant more food for the tribe to eat. Fish were a good source of food, and traveling by boat was often easier than walking long distances. Water was needed in every part of tribal life.

Village and tribelet land was carefully guarded. Each group knew exactly where the boundaries of its land were found. Boundaries were known by landmarks such as mountains or rivers, or they might also be marked by poles planted in the ground. Some boundary lines were marked by rocks, or by objects placed there by tribal members. The size of a territory had to be large enough to supply food to every person living there.

The California tribes spoke many languages. **Sometimes** villages close together even had a problem understanding one another. This meant that each group had to be sure of the boundaries of other tribes around them when gathering food. It would not be wise to go against the boundaries and the customs of neighbors. The Native Americans found if they respected the boundaries of their neighbors, not so many wars had to be fought. California tribes, in spite of all their differences, were not as warlike as other tribes in our country.

Not only did the California tribes speak different languages, but their members also differed in size. Some tribes were very tall, almost six feet tall. The shortest people came from the Yuki tribe which had territory in what is now Mendocino County. They measured only about 5'2" tall. All Native Americans, regardless of size, had strong, straight black hair and dark brown eyes.

TRADE

Trading between tribes was an important part of life. Inland tribes had large animal hides that coastal tribes wanted. By trading the hides to coastal groups, inland tribes would receive fish and shells, which they in turn wanted. Coastal tribes also wanted minerals and rocks mined in the mountains by inland tribes. Obsidian rock from the northern mountains was especially wanted for arrowheads. There were, as well, several minerals, mined in the inland mountains, which could be made into the colorful body paints needed for religious ceremonies.

Southern tribes particularly wanted steatite from the Gabrielino tribe. Steatite, or soapstone, was a special metal which allowed heat to spread evenly through it. This made it a good choice to be used for cooking pots and flat frying pans. It could be carved into bowls because of its softness and could be decorated by carving designs into it. Steatite came from Catalina Island in the Coastal Gabrielino territory. Gabrielinos found steatite to be a fine trading item to offer for the acorns, deerskins, or obsidian stone they needed.

When people had no items to trade but needed something, they used small strings of shells for money. The small dentalium shells, which came from the far distant Northwest coast, had great value. Strings of dentalia usually served as money in the Northern California tribes, although some dentalia was used in the Central California tribes.

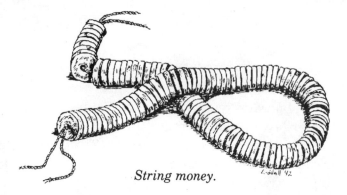

String money.

6

In southern California clam shells were broken and holes were bored through the center of each piece. Then the pieces were rounded and polished with sandstone and strung into strings for money. These were not thought to be as valuable as dentalia.

Strings of shell money were measured by tattoo marks on the trader's lower arm or hand.

Here is a sample of shell value:

A house, three strings
A fishing place, one to three strings
Land with acorn-bearing oak trees, one to five strings

A great deal of rock and stone was traded among the tribes for making tools. Arrows had to have sharp-edged stone for tips. The best stone for arrow tips was obsidian (volcanic glass) because, when hit properly, it broke off into flakes with very sharp edges. California tribes considered obsidian to be the most valuable rock for trading.

Some tribes had craftsmen who made knives with wooden handles and obsidian blades. Often the handles were decorated with carvings. Such knives were good for trading purposes. Stone mortars and pestles, used by the women for grinding grains into flour, were good trading items.

BASKETS & POTTERY

California tribal women made beautiful baskets. The Pomo and Chumash baskets, what few are left, show us that the women of those tribes might have been some of the finest basketmakers in the world. Baskets were used for gathering and storing food, for carrying babies, and even for hauling water. In emergencies, such as flooding waters, sometimes children, women, and tribal belongings crossed the swollen rivers and streams in huge, woven baskets! Baskets were so tightly woven that not a drop of water could leak from them.

Baskets also made fine cooking pots. Very hot rocks were taken from a fire and tossed around inside baskets with a looped tree branch until food in the basket was cooked.

Most baskets were made to do a certain job, but some baskets were designed for their beauty alone and were excellent for trading. Older women of a tribe would teach young girls how to weave baskets.

Pottery was not used by many California tribes. What little there was seems to have been made by those tribes living near to the Navaho and Mohave tribes of Arizona, and it shows their style. For example, pottery of the California tribes did not have much decoration and was usually a dull red color. Designs were few and always in yellow.

Ohlone hunter wearing deerskin camouflage.

Long thin coils of clay were laid one on top the other. Then the coils were smoothed between a wooden paddle and a small stone to shape the bowl. Pottery from California Native Americans has been described as light weight and brittle (easily broken), probably because of the kind of clay soil found in California.

HUNTING & FISHING

Tribal men spent much of their time making hunting and fishing tools. Bows and arrows were built with great care, to make them shoot as accurately as possible. Carelessly made hunting weapons caused fewer animals to be killed and people then had less food to eat.

Bows made by men of Southern California tribes were made long and narrow. In the northern part of the state bows were a little shorter, thinner, and wider than those of their northern neighbors. Size and thickness of bows depended on the size trees growing in a tribe's territory. The strongest bows were wrapped with sinew, the name given to animal tendons. Sinew is strong and elastic like a rubber band.

Arrows were made in many sizes and shapes, depending on their use. For hunting larger animals, a two-piece arrow was used. The front piece of the arrow shaft was made so that it would remain in the animal, even if the back part

9

was removed or broken off. The arrowhead, or point, was wrapped to the front piece of the shaft. This kind of arrow was also used in wars.

Young boys used a simple wooden arrow with the end sharpened to a point. With this they could hunt small animals like birds and rabbits. The older men of the tribe taught boys how to make their own arrows, how to aim properly, and how to repair broken weapons.

Tribal men spent many hours making and mending fishing nets. The string used in making nets often came from the fibers of plants. These fibers were twisted to make them strong and tough, then knotted into netting. Fences, or weirs, that had one small opening for fish, were built across streams. As the fish swam through the opening they would be caught in netting or harpooned by a waiting fisherman.

Hooks, if used at all, were cut from shells. Mostly hooks could be found when the men fished in large lakes or when catching trout in high mountain areas. Hooks were attached to heavy plant fiber string.

Dip nets, made of netting attached to branches that were bent into a circle, were used to catch fish swimming near shore. Dip nets had long handles so the fishermen could reach deep into the water.

Sometimes a mild poison was placed on the surface of shallow water. This confused the fish and caused them to float to the surface of the water, where they could be scooped up by a waiting fisherman. Not enough poison was used to make humans ill.

Not all fishing was done from the shore. California tribes used two kinds of boats when fishing. Canoes, dug out of one half a log, were useful for river fishing. These were square at each end, round on the bottom, and very heavy. Some of them were well-finished, often even having a carved seat in them.

Today we think of "balsa" as a very lightweight wood, but in Spanish, the word balsa means "raft". That is why Spanish explorers called the Native American canoes, made from tule reeds, "balsa" boats.

Balsa boats were made of bundled tule reeds and were used throughout most of California. They made into safe, light-weight boats for lake and river use. Usually the balsa canoe had a long, tightly tied bundle of tule for the boat bottom and one bundle for each side of the canoe. The front of the canoe was higher than the back. Balsa boats could be steered with a pole or with a paddle, like a raft.

Men did most of the fishing, women were in charge of gathering grasses, seeds, and acorns for food. After the food was collected, it was either eaten right away or made ready for winter storage.

Except for a few southern groups, California tribes had permanent villages where they lived most of the year. They also had food-gathering places they returned to each year to collect acorns, salt, fish, and other foods not found near their villages.

FOOD

Many different kinds of plant food grew wild in California in the days before white people arrived. Berries and other plant foods grew in the mountains. Forests offered the local tribes everything from pine nuts to animals.

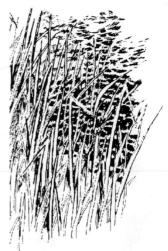

Native Americans found streams full of fish for much of the year. Inland fresh water lakes had large tule reeds growing along their shores. Tule could be eaten as food when plants were young and tender. More important,

11

however, tule was used in making fabric for clothes and for building boats and houses. Tule was probably the most useful plant the California Native Americans found growing wild in their land.

Like all deserts, the one in southern California had little water or fish, but small animals and cactus plants made good food for the local tribes. They moved from place to place harvesting whatever was ripe. Tribal members always knew when and where to find the best food in their territory.

Acorns were the main source of food for all California tribes. Acorn flour was as important to the California Native Americans as wheat is to us today. Five types of California oak trees produced acorns that could be eaten. Those from black oak and tanbark oak seem to have been the favorite kinds.

Since some acorns tasted better than others, the tastiest ones were collected first. If harvest of the favorite acorn was poor some years, then less tasty acorns had to be eaten all winter long.

So important were acorns to California Indians that most tribes built their entire year around them. Acorn harvest marked the beginning of their calendar year. Winter was counted as so many months after acorn harvest, and summer was counted by the number of months before the next acorn harvest.

Acorn harvest ceremonies usually were the biggest events of the year. Most celebrations took place in mid-October and included dancing, feasts, games of chance, and reunions with relatives. Harvest festivals lasted for many days. They were a time of joy for everyone.

The annual acorn gathering lasted two to three weeks. Young boys climbed the oak trees to shake branches; some men used long poles to knock acorns to the ground. Women loaded the nuts into large cone-shaped burden baskets and carried them to a central place where they were put in the sun to dry.

Once the acorns were dried, the women carried them back to the tribe's permanent villages. There they lined special basket-like storage granaries with strong herbs to keep insects away, then stored the acorns inside. Granaries were placed on stilts to keep animals from getting into them and were kept beside tribal houses.

Preparing acorns for each meal was also the women's job. Shells were peeled by hitting the acorns with a stone hammer on an anvil (flat) stone. Meat from the nut was then laid on a stone mortar. A mortar was usually a large stone with a slight dip on its surface. Sometimes the mortar had a bottomless basket, called a hopper, glued to its top. This kept the acorn meat from sliding off the mortar as it was beaten.
The meat was then pounded with a long stone pestle. Acorn flour was scraped away from the hopper's sides with a soaproot fiber brush during this process.

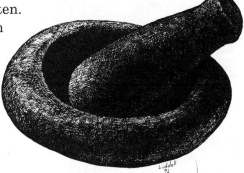

From there the flour was put into an open-worked basket and sifted. A fine flour came through the bottom of the basket, while the larger pieces were put back in the mortar for more pounding.

The most important process came after the acorn flour was sifted. Acorn flour has a very bitter-tasting tannin in it. This bitter taste was removed by a method called leaching. Many tribes leached the flour by first scooping out a hollow in sand near water. The hollow was lined with leaves to keep the flour from washing away. A great deal of hot water was poured through the flour to wash out (leach) the

13

bitterness. Sometimes the flour was put into a basket for the leaching process, instead of using sand and leaves.

Finally the acorn flour was ready to be cooked. To make mush, heated stones were placed in the basket with the flour. A looped tree branch or two long sticks were used to toss the hot rocks around so the basket would not burn. When the mush had boiled, it could be eaten. If the flour and water mixture was baked in an earthen oven, it became a kind of bread. Early explorers wrote that it was very tasty.

Historians have estimated that one family would eat from 1500 to 2000 pounds of acorn flour a year. One reason California native Americans did not have to plant seeds and raise crops was because there were so many acorns for them to harvest each year.

Whether they ate fish or shellfish or plant food or animal meat, nature supplied more than enough food for the Native Americans who lived in California long ago. Many believed their good fortune in having fine weather and plenty to eat came from being good to their gods.

RELIGION

Tribal members had strong beliefs in the power of spirits or gods around them. Each tribe was different, but all felt the importance of never making a spirit angry with them. For that reason a celebration to thank the spirit-gods for treating them well, took place before each food gathering and before each hunting trip, and after each food harvest.

Usually spiritual powers were thought to belong to birds or animals. Most California tribespeople felt bears were very wicked and should not be eaten. But Coyote seems to have been a kind leader who helped them if they were in trouble, even though he seems to have been a bit naughty at times. Eagle was thought to be very powerful and good to native Americans. In some tribes, Eagle was almost as powerful as Sun.

Tribes placed importance on different gods, according to the tribe's needs. Rain gods were the most important spirits to desert tribes. Weather gods, who might bring less rain or warmer temperatures, were important to northern tribes. A great many groups felt there were gods for each of the winds: North, South, East and West. The four directions were usually included in their ceremonial dances and were used as part of the decorations on baskets, pots, and even tools.

Animals were not only worshipped and believed to be spirit-gods, like Deer or Antelope, but tribal members felt there was a personal animal guardian for each one of them. If a tribal member had a deer as guardian, then that person could never kill a deer or eat deer meat.

California Native Americans believed in life after death. This made them very respectful of death and very fearful of angering a dead person. Once someone died, the name of the dead person could never again be said aloud. Since it was easy to accidentally say a name aloud, the name was usually given to a new baby. Then the dead person would not become angry.

Shamans were thought to be the keepers of religious beliefs and to have the ability to talk directly to spirit-gods. It was the job of a village shaman to cure sick people, and to speak to the gods about the needs of the people. Some tribes had several kinds of shamans in one village. One shaman did curing, one scared off evil spirits, while another took care of hunters.

Not all shamans were nice, so people greatly feared their power. However, if shamans had no luck curing sick people or did not bring good luck in hunting, the people could kill them. Most shamans were men, but in a few tribes, women were doctors.

Most California tribal myths have been lost to history because they were spoken and never written down. The legends were told and retold on winter nights around the home fires. Sadly, these were forgotten after the missionaries brought Christianity to California and moved tribal members into the missions.

A few stories still remain, however. It is thought by historians that northwest California tribes were the only ones not to have a myth on how they were created. They did not feel that the world was made and prepared for human beings. Instead, their few remaining stories usually tell of mountain peaks or rivers in their own territory.

The central California tribes had creation stories of a great flood where there was only water on earth. They tell of how man was made from a bit of mud that a turtle brought up from the bottom of the water.

Many southwest tribes believed there was a time of no sky or water. They told of two clouds appearing which finally became Sky and Earth.

Throughout California, however, all tribes had myths that told of Eagle as the leader, Coyote as chief assistant, and of less powerful spirits like Falcon or Hawk.

Costumes for religious ceremonies often imitated these animals they worshipped or feared. Much time was spent in making the dance costumes as beautiful as possible. Red woodpecker feathers were so brilliant a color they were used to decorate religious headdresses, necklaces, or belts. Deerskin clothing was fringed so shell beads could be attached to each thin strip of leather.

Eagle feathers were felt to be the most sacred of religious objects. Sometimes they were made into whole robes.

Religious feather charm.

Usually, though, the feathers were used just for decorations. All these costumes were valuable to the people of each tribe. The village chief was in charge of taking care of the costumes, and there was terrible punishment for stealing them. Clothing worn everyday was not fancy like costuming for rituals.

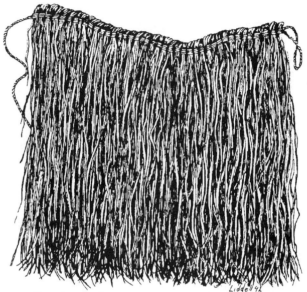

Willow bark skirt.

CLOTHING

Central and southern California's fine weather made regular clothes not really very important to the Native Americans. The children and men went naked most of the year, but most women wore a short apron-like skirt. These skirts were usually made in two pieces, front and back aprons, with fringes cut into the bottom edges. Often the skirt was made from the inner bark of trees, shredded and gathered on a cord. Sometimes the skirt was made from tule or grass.

In northern California and in rainy or windy weather elsewhere in the state, animal-skin blankets were worn by both men and women. They were used like a cape and wrapped around the body. Sometimes the cape was put over one shoulder and under the other arm, then tied in front. All kinds of skins were used; deer, otter, wildcat, but sea-otter fur was thought to be the best. If the skin was from a small animal, it was cut into strips and woven together into a fabric. At night the cape became a blanket to keep the person warm.

Because of the rainy weather in northern California, the women wore basket caps all the time. Women of the central and south tribes wore caps only when carrying heavy loads, where the forehead had to be used as support. Then a cap helped keep too much weight from being placed on the forehead.

Most California people went barefoot in their villages. For journeys into rough land, going to war, wood gathering, or in colder weather, the tribesmen in central and northwest California wore a one-piece soft shoe with no extra sole, which went high up on the leg.

Southern California tribespeople, however, wore sandals most of the time, wearing high, soled moccasins only when they traveled long distances or into the mountains. Leggings of skin were worn in snow, and moccasins were sometimes lined with grass for more comfort and warmth.

VILLAGE LIFE

Houses of the California tribes were made of materials found in their area. Usually they were round with a domed roofs. Except for a few tribes, a house floor was dug into the earth a few feet. This was wise, for it made the home warmer in winter and cooler in summer. It also meant that less material was needed to make house walls.

Framework for the walls was made from bendable branches tied to support poles. Some frames of the houses were covered with earth and grass. Others were covered with large slabs of redwood or pine bark. Central California

Split-stick clapper, rhythm instrument. Hupa tribe.

villagers made large woven mats of tule reed to cover the tops and sides of houses. In the warmer southern area, brush and smaller pieces of bark were used for house walls.

Most California Native American villages had a building called a sweathouse, where the men could be found when they were not hunting, fishing or traveling. It was a very important place for the men, who used it rather like a clubhouse. They could sweat and then scrape themselves clean with curved ribs of deer. The sweathouse was smaller than a family house. Normally it had a center pole framework with a firepit on the ground next to the pole. When the fire was lit, some smoke was allowed to escape through a hole at the top of the roof; however, most was trapped inside the building. Smoke and heat were the main reasons for having a sweathouse. Both were believed to be a way to purify tribal members' bodies. Sweathouse walls were mainly hard-packed earth. The heat produced was not a steam heat but came from a wood-fed fire.

In the center of most villages was a large house that often had no walls, just a roof held up with poles. It was here that religious dances and rituals were held, or visitors were entertained.

Dances were enjoyed and were performed with great skill. Music, usually only rhythm instruments, accompanied the dances. For some reason California Native Americans did not use drums to create rhythms for their dances. Three different kinds of rattles were used by California tribes.

One type, split-clap sticks, created rhythm for dancing. These were usually a length of cane (a hollow stick) split in half lengthwise for about two-thirds of its length. The part still uncut was tightly wound with cord so it would not split all the way. The stick was held at the tied end in one hand and hit against the palm of the other hand to make its sound.

A pebble-filled moth cocoon made rhythm for shaman duties. These could range from calling on spirits to cure illnesses, to performing dances to bring rain. Probably the best sounds to beat rhythm for songs and dances came from bundles of deer hooves tied together on a stick. These rattles have a hollow, warm sound.

The only really "musical" instrument found in California was a flute made of reed that was played by blowing across the edge of one end. Melodies were not played on any of these instruments. Most North American Indians sang their songs rather than playing melodies on music instruments.

Special songs were sung for each event. There were songs for healing sick people, songs for success in hunting, war, or marriage. Women sang acorn-grinding songs and lullabies. Songs were sung in sorrow for the dead and during story-telling times. Group singing, with a leader, was the favorite kind of singing. Most songs were sung by all tribe members, but religious songs had to be sung by a special group. It was important that sacred songs not be changed through the years. If a mistake was made while singing sacred music, the singer could be punished, so only specially trained singers would sing ritual songs.

All songs were very short, some of them only 20 to 30 seconds long. They were made longer by repeating the melodies over and over, or by connecting several songs together. Songs usually told no story, just repeated words or phrases or syllables in patterns.

Song melodies used only one or two notes and harmony was never added. Perhaps that is why mission Indians, at those missions with musician priests, especially loved to sing harmony in the church choirs.

Songs and dances were good methods of passing rich tribal traditions on to the children. It was important to tribal adults that their children understand and love the tribe's heritage.

Children were truly wanted by parents in most tribes and new parents carefully watched their tiny babies day and night, to be sure they stayed warm and dry. Usually a newborn was strapped into a cradle and tied to the mother's back so she could continue to work, yet be near the baby at all times. In some tribes, older children took care of babies of cradle age during the day to give the mother time to do all her work, while grandmothers were often in charge of caring for toddlers.

Children were taught good behavior, traditions, and tribal rules from babyhood, although some tribes were stricter than others. Most of the time parents made their children obey. Young children could be lightly punished, but in many tribes those over six or seven years old were more severely punished if they did not follow the rules.

Just as children do today, Native American youngsters had childhood traditions they followed. For instance, one tribal tradition said that when a baby tooth came out, a child waited until dusk, faced the setting sun and threw the tooth to the west. There is no mention of a generous tooth fairy, however.

Tribal parents were worried that their offspring might not be strong and brave. Some tribes felt one way to make their children stronger was by forcing them to bathe in ice cold water, even in wintertime. Every once in a while, for example, Modoc children were awakened from sleep and taken to a cold lake or stream for a freezing bath.

But if freezing baths at night were hard on young Native Americans, their days were carefree and happy. Children were allowed to play all day, and some tribes felt children did not even have to come to dinner if they didn't want to. In those tribes, children could come to their houses to eat anytime of the day.

The games boys played are not too different from those played today. Swimming, hide and seek among the tule reeds, a form of tetherball with a mud ball tied to a pole, and willow-javelin throwing kept boys busy throughout the day.

Fathers made their sons small bows and arrows, so boys spent much time trying to improve their hunting skills. They practised shooting at frogs or chipmunks. The first animal any boy killed was not touched or eaten by him. Others would carry the kill home to be cooked and eaten by villagers. This tradition taught boys always to share food.

Another hunting tool for boys was a hollowed-out willow branch. This became like a modern day beanshooter, only the Native American boys shot juniper berries instead of beans. Slingshots made good hunting weapons, as well.

Girls and boys shared many games, but girls playing with each other had contests to see who could make a basket the fastest, or they played with dolls made of tule. Together, young boys and girls played a type of ring-around-the-rosie game, climbed mountains, or built mud houses.

As children grew older, the boys followed their fathers and the girls followed their mothers as the adults did their daily work. Children were not trained in the arts of hunting or basketmaking, however, until they became teenagers.

HISTORY

Spanish missionaries, led by Fray Junipero Serra, arrived in California in 1769 to build missions along the coast of California. By 1823, fifty years later, 21 missions had been founded. Almost all of them were very successful, and the Franciscan monks who ran them were proud of how many Native Americans became Christians.

However, all was not as the monks had planned it would be. Native American people had never been around the diseases European white men brought with them. As a result, they had no immunity to such illnesses as measles, small pox, or flu. Too many mission Indians died from white men's diseases.

Historians figure there were 300,000 Native Americans living in California before the missionaries came. The missions show records of 83,000 mission Indians during mission days. By the time the Mexicans took over the missions from the Spanish in 1834, only 20,000 remained alive.

The great California Gold Rush of 1849 was probably another big reason why many of the Native Americans died during that time. White men, staking their claim to tribal lands with gold upon it, thought nothing of killing any California tribesman who tried to keep and protect his territory. Fifty-thousand tribal members died from diseases, bullets, or starvation between the gold Rush Days and 1870. By 1910, only 17,000 California Indians remained.

Although the American government tried to set aside reservations (areas reserved for Native Americans), the land given to the Indians often was not good land. Worse yet, some of the land sacred to tribes, such as burial grounds, was taken over by white people and never given back.

Sadly, mission Indians, when they became Christians, forgot the proud heritage and beliefs they had followed for thousands of years. Many wonderful myths and songs they had passed from one generation to the next, on winter nights so long ago, have been lost forever.

Today some 100,000 people can claim California Native American ancestors, but few pure-blooded tribespeople remain. Our link with the Wanderers, who came from Asia so long ago, has been forever broken.

The bullroarer made a deep, loud sound when whirled above the player's head. Tipai tribe.

Villages were usually built beside a lake, stream, or river. Balsa canoes are on the shore. Tule reeds grow along the edge of the water and are drying on poles on the right side of the picture.

Women preparing food in baskets, sit on tule mats. Tule mats are being tied to the willow pole framework of a house being built by one of the men.

GABRIELINO TRIBE

People who have studied the history of California Native Americans believe that the Gabrielino (Gob ree el een' oh) tribe was possibly the richest, largest, and most powerful tribe in Southern California.

Spanish explorers, who wrote about the Gabrielinos in their journals, found them to be very smart when dealing with neighboring tribes. They were physically strong people, medium height, stocky build, and had skin of such a light color that Spanish explorers called them "white" Indians. The women may have appeared lighter colored; they protected their skin from browning and wrinkling by using red ochre paint on their bodies, much as we use sun shade today.

The name Gabrielino came from historians, not from the people themselves. The word Gabrielino meant Indians of the San Gabriel Mission, which was founded in the year 1771. Before that time the tribe had no name for itself.

Today, people with Gabrielino ancestors (long-ago relatives) are searching for a new name for themselves. They want a name which best describes the people and the land as it used to be. Some Gabrielinos think the name Tongva, which means, "earth" in their ancient language, would be a good name.

The Gabrielinos lived in an area which is mainly Los Angeles and Orange Counties today. The Fernandiño tribe's territory was in the San Fernando Valley just north of the Gabrielinos. The tribe became mission Indians at Mission San Fernando Rey de España about twenty years after the Gabrielinos became a part of Mission San Gabriel. Territory of the two tribes was side by side, and they both spoke the same language. Since the tribes also had the same kind of land, plants and climate, their foods, weapons and trading items were nearly the same.

Their land had four major kinds of climate:

1. Mountains and foothills – It was an area of many small animals, deer, acorns, sagebrush, piñon nuts, and many plant foods good to eat.

2. Prairie – Acorns, sage, yucca, cactus, and other plant foods, as well as large animals like deer, small rodents (rabbits and rats), many kinds of birds were found in this part of the Gabrielino-Fernandino territory. Because so many streams of fresh water and marshlands were here, the area was a fine place to live.

3. Exposed coast – There were no trees on the land, and ocean winds blew constantly. No villages were found there, but food-gathering camps were found everywhere. Much important food, such as shellfish and kelp, was gathered. Swordfish, shark, and tuna were caught in the close-to-shore ocean waters.

4. Sheltered coast – This land had small trees, hills, and canyons which protected people and plants from the winds. Many villages were built there and many food plants, as well as sea animals and fish, gave the people plenty to eat.

Gabrielino territory went from the southern tip of the San Fernando Valley in the north to Newport Bay in the south. The land stretched east to where the city of San Bernardino is today.

There was snow in the mountains each winter, and the lower land had delightful weather throughout most of the year. Sometimes the summers had 100° temperatures, but most of the time summer weather was between 75° and 85°.

Islands belonging to the Gabrielinos were just off the coast. A few had no animal or plant life, but many seals, sea lions, and sea otters, as well as sea birds could be found on most of the islands. Santa Catalina Island had deer, and some plant life was found there. However, the island had one valuable mineral which could be easily mined: steatite. This rock was very valuable to the Gabrielinos. It is a soft rock, (we call it soapstone), and it was needed by most southern California tribes for cooking utensils. A great deal of the Gabrielino wealth came from the trading of this rock for many fine objects they wanted. Tribal members knew their land well, so could make good use of the plants, rocks, and climate of their territory.

THE VILLAGE

Most villages were separate from one another, and each took care of its own needs. Some people owned land within the villages. Boundaries of land owned by one person were marked by painting the personal tattoo of an owner on trees or rocks.

The houses were round with rounded, or domed, roof. Walls were made of woven tule, fern, or grass. Houses near the ocean had doors which opened westward toward the sea, so the cold north wind would not blow inside.

Since villages were mostly made up of groups of people related to each other, many homes were built large enough to hold big families. Explorers' journals noted that some houses were so large they could hold fifty people at one time. Houses on Catalina Island were found to be 60 feet across at floor level with signs of three or four families having lived in them.

Each village had a small earth-covered building which was shaped like one of the domed houses cut in half. This semicircular building was called a sweathouse, but was used by the men of the village for more than just a place to sweat their bodies clean. It was also a clubhouse or meeting place for men.

There was a ceremonial area close to the village chief's house. This was an open-air, fenced place for religious

Tall tule reeds.

ceremonies, and for dancing. It was oval in shape, with walls made of willow branches woven in and out between willow stakes. The dance enclosure was decorated with eagle and raven feathers, animal skins, and flowers.

Often there was a second building near the sacred dance enclosure. It was shaped like the enclosure, but was not religious or sacred. This place was used by villagers to practice the ceremonies and dances to be presented in the sacred ceremonial enclosure.

Although the tribe moved to different places while gathering foods during the summer and fall, tribal members always came back to their permanent village.

VILLAGE LIFE

Gabrielinos expected their children to be truthful at all times. Children were also taught to be kind to old people and to care for them. As young adults they were taught to respect the in-laws of their husbands or wives. All tribal members believed that those people who always followed the tribal laws would live long, happy lives.

There were three different kinds of people found in a village. Most important were the very rich tribal members, and the chief and his or her family. Just below this group of people were the rather well-to-do and long-time families of the village. Everyone else, mostly workers, was included in the lower group of villagers.

The Gabrielinos were an intelligent tribe. They had divided their year into two parts, with ten moons (months). They had named many stars, usually giving them animal names. The tribe also had names for north, south, east, and west.

A village far away from any neighbors was usually ruled by its own chief. However, sometimes there were several villages very close together. These villages might choose to have one chief in charge of all of them. For instance, San Pedro (called "place of the skies" by Native Americans) was the center for several nearby villages. One chief was chosen to be leader of all of them. This chief lived in San Pedro because it was the largest village.

When an old chief died, the eldest son usually became chief. Villagers expected the son to be as fine a leader as his father had been. If the son was thought not to have good enough behavior, or if the chief had no son, then a new chief was chosen by the village council from among the chief's relatives. If there was no male relative worthy of being leader, a woman (usually a sister or daughter of the old chief) was chosen.

Village chiefs were in charge of the sacred bundle, which held holy symbols of their tribe's religious beliefs. Their most important job, besides caring for the sacred bundle, was to keep tribal members in one united group. In order to do this, chiefs had to settle problems between villagers. They had to set good examples by being very good people. A chief also was in charge of collecting taxes. Tribelet chiefs not only led their people into war but arranged peace treaties at war's end.

A chief had several assistants who handled such jobs as being a village announcer, the treasurer, or being a chief's messenger. Messengers had to have excellent memories, since there was no written language for sending notes to distant villages. Because they carried the word of the chief, messengers were especially well trained and stayed in their jobs until their abilities to remember things began to fail.

Earth oven. Food was wrapped in leaves
or clay before being baked in the oven.

Announcers were masters of ceremonies at festivals and announced news to the villagers. A treasurer took care of village taxes, which were not payments of money, but were mostly food gifts given to the chief to feed visitors.

A chief also had a general assistant whose particular job was to give long talks to the villagers about their behavior. As in many California tribes, good behavior was expected from every tribal member from the time they were born.

When a baby was born, the mother and her child were purified by sweatbathing for three days after the baby's birth. If the new baby was a chief's child, a special ritual was held. The baby received a ceremonial bathing, and older women of the village danced as they foretold greatness in the future of the newborn child.

For the first year of its life, the baby's bed was a cradle made of wood. It looked like a U-shaped ladder and had an animal skin hood. Women carried their babies on their backs with nettings worn across their foreheads to hold the cradles in place. Sometimes, however, the baby was held in a carrying net, like a hammock, on the mother's back.

Gabrielino parents treated their children with such love and devotion, that mission priests were amazed. The priests wrote of children being treated like "little idols". However, children were also taught good manners. From an early age, they were made to show respect for anyone older than they were. They learned not to walk or run between two adults and were never allowed to interrupt an adult conversation.

It was the job of the older men and women of the tribe to train the older children in the chores and crafts of the tribe. Old men taught boys how to make bows and arrows, how to make fish nets, and how to hunt and fish. Old women showed girls how to gather and prepare foods, and how to make clothing.

Little is known about ceremonies performed for boys becoming teenagers, but girls were given large and grand ceremonies as they passed into the teenage years. At her own ceremony, a girl was the center of attention. All dancing and singing was done in her honor.

During this joyful time, a sand painting was made for the young girl that showed certain supernatural beings of the universe. Meanings of the sand painting were taught to her so she could better understand her place in the whole universe.

Time was given at this ceremony to teach the teenage girl proper womanly behavior. Each girl was told she must work hard throughout her life, must bathe every day, and must always tell the truth. At the end of the ceremony, the new teenager was presented as a woman to her own people and to visiting tribelets.

Sometimes parents would arrange a marriage for their children when they were still quite small. More often, young people picked their own husbands or wives after they became teenagers.

When a young man and woman were sure they were suited for each other, the Gabrielino customs for a marriage were followed. Men of the groom's family would travel to the bride-to-be's village and visit her home. These visitors brought gifts of shell beads to present to her family. A few days later, the bride-to-be's family would journey to the groom's home with gifts of food. A date for the wedding would be set. On her wedding day, the bride was dressed in soft skins and feathers. Her body was painted. When she was ready, her relatives carried her toward the groom's house. Friends and neighbors of her village would follow her, all the while singing, dancing, and carrying gifts. Halfway there the groom's relatives would meet the procession. His family would then carry the bride the rest of the way to the groom's village.

When the bride arrived at the groom's village, she was seated next to the groom. Baskets of seeds were poured over the new husband and wife to make sure their future together would be full of riches and good fortune. A festive dance followed, with warriors and hunters dancing in full costumes.

From that day forward, the bride could not visit her relatives, but the relatives could always visit her. The young couple worked together to have a healthy family. The man would hunt and fish for food and the woman cared for children and prepared food the husband had provided. It was a busy life.

Gabrielinos believed that when important persons died they would rise to the heavens and become stars. Ordinary people were thought to go underground when they died. There they would dance and feast forevermore.

Mainland Gabrielinos wrapped bodies in blankets used by the dead persons during their lifetimes. Relatives would then cry a ritual wail and dance as they wailed. After three days of mourning the loss of their relative, tribal members

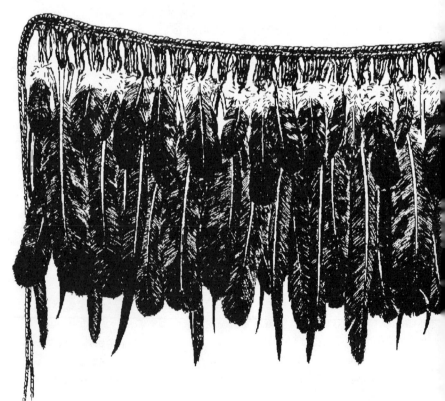

Dance skirt of eagle feathers.

would burn the body along with most of the dead person's belongings.

Those belongings not burned were saved for the annual mourning ceremony. It is thought that Gabrielinos may have been the first tribe in California to hold a large mourning ceremony. It was certainly the biggest event of the year for the Gabrielinos. Held in the autumn just after the acorn harvest, the ceremony was not only for villagers. Guests from other villages were invited as well. Eight days were spent teaching tribal members the ceremonial rituals, songs, and dances to be performed at the actual ceremony.

For seven days after the ceremony began, there was visiting with guests, dancing, singing, and feasting. Dancers acted out religious times of the past. A shaman-priest, who had

taught the dancers all their steps, watched on the sidelines to be sure no mistakes were made. Costumes for the dancers were quite beautiful. Hawk and eagle feathers were used as decorations, and the dancers' faces and necks gleamed with bright paint.

On the fourth day of the event, all new babies born during the year were given their names at a special ceremony. It was the chief's job to name each child, and he chose names which came from the child's ancestors.

On the important fifth day, life-size images were made of those who had died. These mourning images were stuffed with grasses to make them look as lifelike as possible. Images of men were decorated with bows and arrows. Women's images had baskets attached to them. On the evening of the fifth day, or on the sixth day, an eagle-killing ceremony was held. Special songs and dances were performed at the eagle ceremony.

Early on the morning of the eighth day the images were carried into the dance enclosure by the dancers as they performed. A huge fire had been built in the enclosure so the dancers could throw the death images into the flames. Along with the images, all dead persons' belongings saved at burials throughout the year were also tossed into the fire.

WAR

Gabrielinos were not afraid to state their opinions to other tribal members or even other tribes. As a result, war was probably not an unusual event to the tribelets. The finding of reed armor, war clubs, swords, and large warfare-type bows and arrows around village archaeological diggings seems to prove the fact that many wars were fought. Although it is not known for sure, there was probably a war chief on most village chiefs' councils.

Wars could come about for such insults as a visiting chief not giving a gift in return for a gift given to him. Trespassing could also cause a war. If the threat of a war came up, all villages involved in the problem would meet to try to work out how the problem could be solved without going to war. Great care was given in reaching a decision to go to war, because a whole village took part in it.

If war was decided upon, the chief would lead every villager to the place of battle, even children. Bows and arrows and war clubs were the weapons used. During the battle, women would rush to pick up all arrows which fell on their side of the line, so the arrows could be shot back in the direction from which they came. Food carried to the battlefield was prepared by the women to keep the warriors from getting hungry. These wars were usually fierce but short.

HUNTING AND FISHING

Men did most of the heavy work of the tribelets. Their important concerns were making sure the homes they built were strong and warm in cold and windy weather, and providing their families with enough food. Although women had the largest job of gathering seeds, roots, and nuts, men did some gathering. Mainly, however, men were the hunters and fishermen in the family.

Large land animals, such as deer or mountain lions, were usually hunted with bows and arrows. The men made all-wood bows about four-and-a-half feet long. The string of the bow was either made from sinew or strong vegetable fiber.

Arrows were usually made of cane. Boys used a one-piece arrow which had no point attached to it; the end was simply sharpened into a point. Sometimes, poison was put on the points. Most hunters' arrows were two-piece with a foreshaft of hardwood. These two-piece arrows were very well-made. The main shaft was hollow reed. At one end there were three hawk feathers inset to guide the arrow in a straight line, when it was shot. At the other end, the cane was dug out to form a pocket. The foreshaft was smaller around and one end of it was fit into the pocket. Points of stone or bone were attached to the other end of the foreshaft. When an animal was shot, the foreshaft would remain in the animal, but the main shaft could be used again.

Rabbits, rats, and other small animals were usually caught in traps, snares, and deadfalls. A deadfall was a type of trap in which a heavy rock would be placed on a platform held up by a slender stick. Food would be put under the platform as bait. When a small bird or animal reached toward the bait, the stick would fall and the weighted platform would kill it.

Gophers and moles were smoked out of their underground homes and killed with a club. Some rabbits were killed with bows and arrows. When many hunters worked together,

Plank canoe, called tomol, used to cross the ocean channel to Catalina Island.

rabbits could be caught in nets held by the hunters. Young boys were trained to be hunters by first learning to shoot at rabbits.

Ocean fishing meant catching large fish. The men used harpoons, spears, and clubs to kill sea lions and large fish. The Gabrielinos were one of only two California tribes (the other tribe was the Chumash tribe) which built sea-going canoes. This strong boat was made of planks of wood which were stitched together with strong milkweed fibers. Tar, or asphaltum, was used to seal between the planks. Trips to Santa Catalina Island were made in this kind of boat.

Most fishing was done from the ocean shore, or in fresh-water streams. Hooks and lines, nets, and basket traps were used to catch fish in lakes and streams. Sometimes spears were used to catch larger freshwater fish. If a stream had some quiet pools of water, a mild poison would be floated on top of the water. The fish would lose control of their muscles enough to float to the surface. The fish could then be picked up with the hands.

FOOD

Fish meat might be eaten raw but was usually roasted over the fire. Fish was also preserved for winter food by smoking it. Deer, and other red meat, was smoked for storage or eaten fresh.

Gabrielinos depended on acorns, as did almost all California tribes. Grass seeds, roots of many plants, berries, and nutmeats were prepared into nutritious meals by parching them in a basket over hot coals. Pits from the fruit of wild plum bushes were ground into a flour. The fruits in Gabrielino territory were not very good for eating, but the women used the pits, or seeds, for food. There were plants which could be made into drinks, and there was even a chewing gum made from a plant.

The climate in southern California was not very good for growing berries. There was one kind of blackberry found in marshlands, and growing in the dry chaparral were bitter-tasting currants and thorny gooseberries. New, tender shoots of the yucca plant had a good taste, as did those of wild sage. Cactus fruit was carefully gathered by using tongs.

The type of food went from the meat of beached whales to toasted caterpillars. Every animal of every size, except bear, was cooked (usually) and eaten. Bears were felt to be too much a part of myths and too spiritual to be eaten by many Gabrielinos.

TOOLS AND UTENSILS

Gabrielinos were known for their clever utensils, tools, and beautiful objects of art. Even everyday tools and utensils were decorated with shells inlaid in tar, or with carved designs. Often hard-to-find minerals were inlaid on the outsides of bowls.

Gabrielinos were also very artistic. Lovely carvings of whales and other animals have been found, and even paintings on rocks have been discovered. The Chumash and Gabrielino tribes were the most advanced in art work and toolmaking of all the southern-central California tribes.

Such cooking utensils as stone mortars and metates (Spanish word for pestle) were used every day. Gabrielino pestles were a thing of beauty. The pestle worked so well to grind food that women gave it the name aman, which meant "it's hand."

Stirrers were carved from wood, small shells made fine spoons, and platters for food could be large pieces of bark. Even a small amount of pottery was made by piling coils of clay atop each other, then smoothing

Stone mortar and pestle.

the coils with a paddle. Very few California tribes made any pottery at all, and the Gabrielinos might have made more of it if they had not had steatite containers.

Gabrielino women made wonderful baskets to help them prepare foods. Baskets were used not only for preparing foods, but for storing belongings and for carrying heavy loads. Women supported the heavy, cone-shaped burden baskets on their backs by using a strip of netting on top of a basket cap which they wore down over their foreheads.

Both coiled and twined baskets were made by the women. Twined baskets were often the most loosely woven and were used to beat seeds from the grasses and bushes, and for winnowing. Winnowing was the method used to get rid of all unneeded parts of wild grain, such as the stalk and leaves, leaving only the kernel to grind into flour. Winnowing baskets made the separating of grain from its husk much easier.

Some baskets were sealed with asphalt at the neck and at the bottom so they could carry and store water. Ceremonial baskets were awesome in their great beauty.

A few baskets were still being used for cooking during explorers' times, but

Steatite frying pan. Hole is to pull pan off the fire with a stick.

the steatite, or soapstone, pans were much easier to use in preparing foods. Steatite spread heat evenly, and women did not have to heat rocks and toss them about in baskets to cook food.

Steatite bowls were favorites, also, and many were decorated with beautiful designs. Besides bowls and pans, steatite was made into pipes, beads, and carvings. Some was ground up into baby powder.

Steatite bowl of artistic shape.

The fibers of yucca roots were strong enough to be made into brushes for cleaning pans or brushing hair. Gourds made good dippers, and plates could be large shells or could be carved from wood.

Bones were sharpened for awls (hole-puncher), shoulder blades of animals were used for hide-scrapers, stones were made into pounding tools, and fine, sharp knives were made by inserting obsidian blades into carved wooden handles.

String and cord were made from the stems of plants such as milkweed, yucca, or nettles. All the pulp was scratched off a stalk with very strong fingernails, leaving only the fibers of the stalk. These were then braided or rolled together on a person's thigh, two or more fibers at a time, until it was of the length and size needed.

TRADE

The most important trading item Gabrielinos offered to other tribes was the soapstone, or steatite, rock. One reason the Gabrielino tribe was so rich was the need for steatite by every tribe around them.

It was just luck that made Catalina Island the only place where steatite could be found and mined, but since Catalina Island happened to be in Gabrielino territory, all of the rock belonged to them. It made the tribe wealthy and strong.

Steatite was not the only item Gabrielino people had to trade. Other tribes also needed salt, sea-otter skins, dried fish, and shell beads from the Gabrielinos. Since most of their land was near the ocean, the Gabrielinos were eager to get acorns, certain seeds, obsidian for arrowheads and knife blades, and deerskin from the inland tribes.

Historians say there are signs that trading was going on as early as the years 600-800 A.D. (After Christ was born). It is thought that whenever "money" was needed, strings of olivella beads were used. The strings of "money" were as long as the distance around a man's fist, and often tattoo marks were placed on traders' arms to measure the length of a string.

CLOTHING

Both men and women wore tattoos on their foreheads, not for business reasons but for the sake of beauty. Sometimes the women liked a chin tattoo rather than one on the forehead.

The designs were usually vertical or horizontal lines. Tattoos were done by pricking the skin with a thorn or sharp rock. Charcoal from a yucca cabbage, or juice from certain leaves, was rubbed into the open skin prick. This made a blue-black tattoo on the skin. Girls were tattooed before they became teenagers.

Very little clothing was worn by Gabrielinos most of the year. The Los Angeles Basin climate was almost always warm, and it seldom rained or became too cold for tribal members. Men and children usually went naked. Women wore aprons of deerskin, or the inner bark of willow or cottonwood trees. The inner bark was shredded and then woven into fabric.

When rainy or cool weather did come, the villager men wore short capes of deerskin around their shoulders, or they wore longer rabbit-fur robes. Strips of twisted rabbit fur were sewn together with milkweed- or yucca-fiber thread, to form the robes. Sometimes even tiny bird skins, with the feathers still attached, were pieced together to make a warm cape. Island and coastal Gabrielinos made warm capes of sea-otter skins. At night, the capes became blankets for sleeping.

Unlike any other tribe, the Gabrielino men did the dressing, or curing, of the animal skins to be used for blankets or clothing. The hides, or skins, were treated with animal brains and wood ashes. The hides were then softened by rubbing stones over the skins, which had been laid over a tilted post. Softened animal hides made fine-looking, warm clothing.

Most Gabrielinos went barefoot. Some tribes living in rocky areas wore sandals made of woven yucca fiber; they looked a lot like sandals we wear today. Both milkweed fibers and yucca-plant fibers made good thread for sewing fabric into clothing, or for making sandals.

Gabrielinos bathed each morning before sunup. The wet family would dry around a warm fire while waiting for breakfast to cook.

Men wore their hair long and parted in the middle. Sometimes the hair was braided, but more often it was left hanging straight or pulled into a topknot on the top of the head and held in place with a bone hairpin.

Women wore their hair long and hanging free in the back. They also liked bangs over their foreheads. To keep the hair glossy, once in a while the women would coat their hair with clay. When the clay was completely dry and caked, they would break it off from the hair in large chunks, leaving the hair shiny and black.

Flowers were used by the women to decorate their hair, in long necklaces around their necks (like Hawaiian leis), or tucked in over their ears. All the girls had tiny shell-bead necklaces. Larger beads, such as those made from Catalina soapstone, whalebone, or olivella shells were used as decorations, also. Earrings of cane (hollow stems) were worn by men, while women wore shell rings in their ears, from which feathers hung.

Costumes worn during dances by warriors, chiefs, and shamans were ornate (covered with ornaments). These costumes were far more colorful than everyday clothing. Beautiful bird feathers, called plumage, were used to decorate the costumes. Fur, shells, and beads were sewn on to skins to give them more color. A heavy cord made from human hair was often the base from which feather headdresses were made.

RELIGION

Most dances were religious. They were an important way Native Americans could talk to their spirit-gods. Gabrielinos are thought to have had such strong beliefs in their spirit-gods and in the myths of how they came to be, that their religion spread to other Southern California tribes. The Juaneño and Luiseño tribes, just south of the Gabrielinos, became firm believers in the Gabrielino religion, Chungichnish.

One Gabrielino myth tells of how there was night all the time on earth. Then a brother and sister appeared. The man was above in the Heaven, and the woman was below, on earth. There were no stars, moon, or sun. It took the man and woman six separate creations to make the world, with its animals, earth and sand, rocks, trees and shrubs, herbs and grasses, and finally its people.

So important was their religious belief that the Gabrielinos began doing all rituals exactly the same way each time. Nothing could be changed, or the spirit-gods would be angry. Special religious places, like sacred "temples", were built in each village. These enclosures had decorated poles and banners and usually had an image of Chungichnish inside them. On the ground near the image were sand-paintings with picture symbols of the universe and figures of Sun and Moon.

Only very old men, and the most powerful people such as chiefs and shaman-priests, were allowed to go into the most sacred parts of an enclosure. In other areas of the enclosure long ceremonies were celebrated and offerings were given, not only to Chungichnish, but to Sun and Moon, as well.

Gabrielino beliefs in the power of nature were strong. To them, rainbows brought good luck. Gabrielinos felt a ball of lightning meant very bad luck was coming. Whirlwinds were thought to bring evil spirits with them.

Not only were Sun and Moon very powerful spirits to the tribe, but such animals as Crow-Raven, Owl, and Eagle were important to their beliefs. In fact, Eagle was believed to be the most powerful symbol of the past.

A village chief had power over all but the shamans. Shamans were believed to have such spiritual powers that even the chief, who was in charge of the sacred bundle, could not disobey them. It was thought that shamans got their power from the supernatural spirit-gods they saw in dreams, or from visions while they were in trances.

If a young shaman-in-training saw an animal or an object while he was in a trance, that animal or object would be-

Deer hoof rattle; handle is of vegetable fiber rope; about 11 inches high.

come the trainee's special symbol to which he prayed for help and power. All kinds of objects were used by a shaman to bring forth proof of power. Dried animal skins, odd looking rocks, plant roots, and power wands were believed to be holders of power to cure sick people, or to bring about a successful hunt. Older shamans helped train new ones. When fully trained, a shaman usually stayed in his own village.

Shamans were called upon to bring rain, even turn themselves into animals, if needed. Those shamans who people thought could change into bears were greatly feared. If shamans became too mean, or practiced evil on their own people, the other shamans had a meeting and stripped all the power from the bad shaman.

Women shamans could become too powerful, as well, and could use their powers for evil. One very powerful woman shaman led a fierce battle against the San Gabriel Mission in the late 1700s.

HISTORY

Archaeologists have studies that show the Gabrielinos were not the first people to live in their area. However, diggings have shown that they were in the Los Angeles basin about 500 B.C. (B.C. means before Christ was born.) By the year 500 A.D. (after Christ was born), there were Gabrielino villages built along rivers, streams, and in sheltered areas of the coast.

Historians believe the way of living seen by the explorers in the 1700s had been followed since 1200 A.D. When explorers landed, it is thought there were as many as 5,000 tribal members living in Gabrielino territory.

Today there is still no real home for those of Gabrielino heritage. Perhaps when a modern name is chosen, a place will be set aside at the same time, just for Gabrielinos.

Mission San Gabriel's cemetery has been a place for the burial of tribal members, and a visit there will give you a feeling of being at one with the Gabrielino spirit. It is sad that there is no longer space for burial in the small patio garden.

OUTLINE OF GABRIELINO TRIBE

I. Introduction
   - A. Explorers' descriptions of Gabrielinos
   - B. Gabrielino name
     1. Search for new name
   - C. Mission areas
   - D. Four climate zones
   - E. Territory boundaries
     1. Mainland tribelets
     2. Island tribelet

II. The village
   - A. Individual boundaries
   - B. Houses
     1. Kinds of houses
   - C. Sweathouse
   - D. Ceremonial enclosures

III. Village life
   - A. Three kinds of people in village
   - B. Chiefs
     1. Tribelet (village) chief
     2. Chief of several villages
     3. Inheriting the position of chief
     4. Duties of chief
        a. Job of assistants
   - C. Babies' birth and first year
   - D. Training of children
   - E. Teenage ceremonies
   - F. Marriage
     1. Parents choosing mate for their child
     2. Wedding ceremony
   - G. Death
     1. Rituals
     2. Mourning (image) ceremony

IV. War
   - A. Reasons for war
   - B. Clothing and weapons of war
   - C. Who went to war

V. Hunting and fishing
- A. Hunting weapons
  - 1. Large animals
    - a. Bows and arrows
  - 2. Small animals
    - a. Traps, clubs, slingshots
- B. Fishing
  - 1. Ocean weapons and tools
  - 2. Kinds of boats
  - 3. Stream fishing

VI. Food
- A. Meat and fish
- B. Plants

VII. Tools and utensils
- A. Stone tools
  - 1. Steatite bowl
- B. Wood tools
- C. Pottery
- D. Baskets
  - 1. Kinds of baskets
  - 2. Uses of baskets
- E. Plants
  - 1. Yucca plant roots
  - 2. Gourds
  - 3. Strings and ropes
- F. Bone tools

VIII. Trade
- A. Trading items of Gabrielinos
- B. What Gabrielinos wanted in trade
- C. Shell money

IX. Clothing
- A. Tattoos
- B. Men's and children's clothes
- C. Women's clothing
- D. Rainy weather clothing
  - 1. Animal skins and their processing
- E. Bathing and hairstyles
- F. Religious costumes

X. Religion
  A. Dances
  B. Name of religion and how it spread
  C. Myths of creation of earth
  D. Rituals
  E. Enclosures
      1. Those allowed in sacred parts of enclosure
  F. Kinds of spirit-gods
  G. Shamans
      1. Training of shamans
      2. Sacred objects
      3. Duties of shaman
XI. History
  A. Time of arrival of tribal members
  B. Number of Gabrielinos when explorers arrived
  C. Mission Indians
      1. White men's diseases
      2. Mission life
      3. Mexican take-over of missions
  D. After mission days

GLOSSARY

AWL: a sharp, pointed tool used for making small holes in leather or wood

CEREMONY: a meeting of people to perform formal rituals for a special reason; like an awards ceremony to hand out trophies to those who earned honors

CHERT: rock which can be chipped off, or flaked, into pieces with sharp edges

COILED: a way of weaving baskets which looks like the basket is made of rope coils woven together

DIAMETER: the length of a straight line through the center of a circle

DOWN: soft, fluffy feathers

DROUGHT: a long period of time without water

DWELLING: a building where people live

FLETCHING: attaching feathers to the back end of an arrow to make the arrow travel in a straight line

GILL NET: a flat net hanging vertically in water to catch fish by their heads and gills

GRANARIES: basket-type storehouses for grains and nuts

HERITAGE: something passed down to people from their long-ago relatives

LEACHING: washing away a bitter taste by pouring water through foods like acorn meal

MORTAR: flat surface of wood or stone used for the grinding of grains or herbs with a pestle

PARCHING:	to toast or shrivel with dry heat
PESTLE:	a small stone club used to mash, pound, or grind in a mortar
PINOLE:	flour made from ground corn
INDIAN RESERVATION:	land set aside for Native Americans by the United States government
RITUAL:	a ceremony that is always performed the same way
SEINE NET:	a net which hangs vertically in the water, encircling and trapping fish when it is pulled together
SHAMAN:	tribal religious men or women who use magic to cure illness and speak to spirit-gods
SINEW:	stretchy animal tendons
STEATITE:	a soft stone (soapstone) mined on Catalina Island by the Gabrielino tribe; used for cooking pots and bowls
TABOO:	something a person is forbidden to do
TERRITORY:	land owned by someone or by a group of people
TRADITION:	the handing down of customs, rituals, and belief, by word of mouth or example, from generation to generation
TREE PITCH:	a sticky substance found on evergreen tree bark
TWINING:	a method of weaving baskets by twisting fibers, rather than coiling them around a support fiber

NATIVE AMERICAN WORDS
WE KNOW AND USE

PLANTS AND TREES
hickory
pecan
yucca
mesquite
saguaro

ANIMALS
caribou
chipmunk
cougar
jaguar
opossum
moose

STATES
Dakota – friend
Ohio – good river
Minnesota – waters that
   reflect the sky
Oregon – beautiful water
Nebraska – flat water
Arizona
Texas

FOODS
avocado
hominy
maise (corn)
persimmon
tapioca
succotash

GEOGRAPHY
bayou – marshy body of
   water
savannah – grassy plain
pasadena – valley

WEATHER
blizzard
Chinook (warm, dry wind)

FURNITURE
hammock

HOUSE
wigwam
wickiup
tepee
igloo

INVENTIONS
toboggan

BOATS
canoe
kayak

OTHER WORDS
caucus – group meeting
mugwump – loner politician
squaw – woman
papoose – baby

CLOTHING
moccasin
parka
mukluk – slipper
poncho

BIBLIOGRAPHY

Cressman, L. S. *Prehistory of the Far West.* Salt Lake City, Utah: University of Utah Press, 1977.

Heizer, Robert F., volume editor. *Handbook of North American Indians; California, volume 8.* Washington, D.C.: Smithsonian Institute, 1978.

Heizer, Robert F. and Elsasser, Albert B. *The Natural World of the California Indians.* Berkeley and Los Angeles, CA; London, England: University of California Press, 1980.

Heizer, Robert F. and Whipple, M.A.. *The California Indians.* Berkeley and Los Angeles, CA; London, England: University of California Press, 1971.

Heuser, Iva. *California Indians.* PO Box 352, Camino, CA 95709: Sierra Media Systems, 1977.

Macfarlen, Allen and Paulette. *Handbook of American Indian Games.* 31 E. 2nd Street, Mineola, N.Y. 11501: Dover Publications, 1985.

Murphey, Edith Van Allen. *Indian Uses of Native Plants.* 603 W. Perkins Street, Ukiah, CA 95482: Mendocino County Historical Society, © renewal, 1987.

National Geographic Society. *The World of American Indians.* Washington, DC: National Geographic Society reprint, 1989.

Tunis, Edwin. *Indians.* 2231 West 110th Street, Cleveland, OH: The World Publishing Company, 1959.

Credits:
Island Industries, Vashon Island, Washington 98070
Dona McAdam, Mac on the Hill, Seattle, Washington 98109

Acknowledgements:
Richard Buchen, Research Librarian, Braun Library,
Southwest Museum
Special thanks

TOLOWA
YUROK KAROK
ACHUMAWI
SHASTA
HUPA ATSUGEWI
YUKI
MAIDU-
KONKOW
WESTERN
POMO N.E. POMO
PATWIN
S.E. POMO
SOUTHERN LAKE
POMO MIWOK
COAST
MIWOK
EASTERN
MIWOK
OHLONE
NORTHERN
YOKUTS
OHLONE FOOTHILL
YOKUTS
TUBATULABAL
SALINAN
SOUTHERN
YOKUTS

CHUMASH

GABRIELINO
CAHUILLA
ISLAND
CHUMASH
JUANEÑO - LUISEÑO
ISLAND
GABRIELINO
DIEGUENO
(IPAI - TIPAI)

Map Art: Dona McAdam

*At last, a detailed book on the
Gabrielino Tribe
written just for students*

Mary Null Boulé taught in the California public school system for twenty-five years. Her teaching years made her aware of the acute need for well-researched regional social studies books for elementary school students. This series on the California Native American tribes fills a long-standing need in California education. Ms. Boulé is also author and publisher of *The Missions: California's Heritage.* She is married and the mother of five grown children.

Illustrator Daniel Liddell has been creating artistic replicas of Native American artifacts for several years, and his paintings reflect his own Native American heritage. His paternal grandmother was full-blood Chickasaw.

ISBN: 877599-30-1